Unicorns

Unicorns

Kristin Landon

Ariel Books
Andrews and McMeel
Kansas City

ISBN: 0-8362-3019-1

Library of Congress Catalog
Card Number: 91-77089

Design: Michael Mendelsohn

✤ CONTENTS ✤

⚜ Introduction ⚜

Of all the creatures of myth and legend, the unicorn is unique. Its beauty has inspired artists the world over. Its combination of great strength and great gentleness compels the human imagination. In Western culture, it symbolizes purity and solitude; in Chinese legend, wisdom and good fortune.

In Europe, for centuries almost everyone believed that unicorns really existed. They were described in detail in the books of that time,

along with whales and elephants and giraffes—
creatures far more preposterous than the
sublime unicorn. Most Europeans never saw
any of these extraordinary animals. But some
cathedrals in Europe had, among their
treasures, the horn of a unicorn: a beautiful
ivory spiral, often six or seven feet long. The
horns were real; they existed. They were
sometimes displayed in public. Why not, then,
believe in the unicorns that grew them? Why not
believe in strength, purity, beauty, rarity?

It almost seems, even now, that unicorns
must be real. Perhaps, in a remote and quiet part

of the world, a traveler is stopping at the edge
of a calm pool . . .

In the pearly light of evening, a white creature
with delicate hooves steps silently down to the
water, gently dips its slender spiral horn, and
drinks.

A dream? A wish? A legend? All these, and
more: the unicorn.

Ancient
Unicorns

The Chinese "Ki-Lin"

The oldest references to unicorns come from China; the earliest recorded sighting occurred in 2697 B.C. The Chinese unicorn, or ki-lin, was one of the "four auspicious creatures" of Chinese legend, the others being the phoenix, the tortoise, and the dragon. The ki-lin appeared rarely; it was a visitor from Heaven, a sign of good fortune. It had the body of a deer, the hooves of a horse, and the tail of an ox. Its single horn, in the center of its forehead, was soft and fleshy. The ki-lin was described as "strong of body and virtuous of mind," eating no living thing, refusing even to walk on green grass for fear of crushing a single blade. It usually was seen at the beginning of the reign of a wise emperor. One of them, it is said, appeared at the birth of the great philosopher K'ung Ch'iu (Confucius). It carried in its mouth a piece of jade on which was written a prophecy of the baby's future greatness. Like the Western unicorn, the ki-lin was strong, lived alone rather than in herds, and was difficult, if not impossible, to capture.

☙ The Persian Unicorn ☙

The oldest existing description of a unicorn in Western culture was written around 400 B.C. by Ctesias, a Greek who served as a physician at the court of Darius II, king of Persia. He described the unicorn as living in "India," which was a much more general term at that time. He wrote that unicorns were:

". . . As large as horses, and larger. Their bodies are white, their heads dark red, and their eyes dark blue. They have a horn on the forehead which is about a foot and a half in length. The dust filed from this horn is administered in a potion as a protection against deadly drugs. The base of this horn, for some two hands'-breadth above the brow, is pure white; the upper part is sharp and of a vivid crimson; and the remainder, or middle portion, is black."

Ctesias described the unicorns as fast, powerful runners, swifter even than the fastest horse. When they were captured, their horns could be made into drinking cups, and anyone who drank from the cup would be immune to poison and to some diseases. Ctesias's writings, preserved in Europe during the Dark Ages, had a tremendous influence on the European unicorn legends.

⚜ The Roman "Cartazon" ⚜

Claudius Aelianus, a Roman writing in the third century A.D., described two kinds of unicorn. One was apparently based on Ctesias's description. The other was different—the "cartazon":

"This animal is as large as a full-grown horse, and it has a mane, tawny hair, feet like those of the elephant, and the tail of a goat. It is exceedingly swift of foot. Between its brows there stands a single black horn, not smooth but with certain natural rings, and tapering to a very sharp point. Of all animals, this one has the most dissonant voice. With beasts of other species that approach it the 'cartazon' is gentle, but it fights with those of its own kind, and not only do the males fight naturally among themselves but they contend even against the females and push the contest to the death. The animal has great strength of body, and it is armed besides with an unconquerable horn. It seeks out only the most deserted places and wanders there alone. In the season of rut it grows gentle toward the chosen female and they pasture side by side, but when this time is over he becomes wild again and wanders alone. They say that the young ones are sometimes taken to the king to be exhibited in contests on days of festival, because of their strength, but no one remembers the capture of a single specimen of mature age."

⚜ The Biblical Unicorn ⚜

An old Jewish folk tale said that unicorns died out during the Great Flood because they were too large to fit into Noah's Ark. Another legend has it that the unicorn swam behind the ark, attached to it by a chain.

The unicorn is also mentioned in the King James version of the Bible:

Job 39: "Will the unicorn be willing to serve thee, or abide by thy crib? Canst thou bind the unicorn with his band in the furrow? or will he harrow the valleys after thee?"

Psalm 22: "Save me from the lion's mouth: for thou hast heard me from the horns of the unicorns."

The King James version was based on early Greek translations of the original Hebrew. In these translations, the Greek word was "monokeros," meaning "one-horn." The Bible as it was known in the Middle Ages was also based on those Greek translations. For many of the people, the fact that unicorns were mentioned in the Bible was proof of their existence.

Natural History of the Unicorn

☫ The Medieval "Bestiaries" ☫

Descriptions of wild animals were popular in medieval Europe. Most of these were based on the work of Greek and Roman authors. Some of the descriptions were clearly not just second-hand, but fourth-, or seventh-, or tenth-hand. Even descriptions of real animals could be wildly distorted. But these "bestiaries," as they were known, were the source of most people's knowledge of the habits and appearance of wild animals. Including, of course, the unicorn.

The unicorn described in the oldest books was fierce, dangerous, unconquerable by force:

". . . But the cruelest is the Unicorne, a Monster that belloweth horriblie, bodyed like a Horse, footed like an eliphant, tayled like a Swyne, and headed like a Stagge. His horne sticketh out of the midds of hys forehead, of a wonderful brightness about foure foote long, so sharp, that whatsoever he pusheth at, he striketh it through easily. He is never caught alive; kylled he may be, but taken he cannot be."

Lodovico de Varthema of Bologna, translated in 1576 by Richard Eden, described two unicorns in Mecca (though he does not say clearly that he saw them himself):

". . . The one of them, which is much hygher than the other, yet not much unlyke to a coolt of thyrtye moneths of age, in the forehead groweth only one horne, in maner ryght foorth, of the length of three cubites.* The other is much younger, of the age of one yeere, and lyke a young coolte: the horne of this is of the length of four handfuls. This beast is of the coloure of a horse of weesel coloure, and hath the head lyke an hart, but no long necke, a thynne manne hangynge only on the one side. Theyir legges are thyn and slender, lyke a fawne or hynde. The hoofes of the fore feete are divided in two, much lyke the feet of a Goat. The outwarde part of the hynder feete is very full of heare. This beast doubtless seemeth wylde and fierce, yet tempereth that fiercenesse with a certain comelinesse."

*A cubit was one and a half feet.

❦ The Renaissance Unicorn ❦

As late as 1607, Edward Topsell, in his *Historie of Foure-Footed Beastes*, described unicorns:

". . . These beasts are very swift . . . . They keep for the most part in the desarts, and live solitary in the tops of the Mountaines. There was nothing more horible than the voice or braying of it, for the voice is strained above measure. It fighteth both with the mouth and with the heeles, with the mouth biting like a Lyon, and with the heeles kicking like a Horse. It is a beast of an untamable nature, and therefore the Lord himself in Job saith, that hee cannot bee tyed with any halter, nor yet accustomed to any cratch or stable."

The unicorn was often described as living in India, which at the time included much of central Asia and Tibet. It was also said to live in Ethiopia—in the Mountains of the Moon.

The Jesuit missionary Jeronimo Lobo, who died in 1678, traveled widely in India and Ethiopia. He wrote a manuscript about his travels, which was translated into English by Samuel Johnson. Lobo claimed to have seen a unicorn himself:

". . . In the Province of Agaus has been seen the Unicorn, that Beast so much talk'd of and so little known; the prodigious Swiftness with which this Creature runs from one Wood into another has given me no Opportunity of examining it particularly, yet I have had so near a sight of it as to be able to give some Description of it. The Shape is the same as that of a beautiful Horse, exact and nicely proportion'd, of a Bay Colour, with a black Tail, which in some Provinces is long, in others very short; some have long Manes hanging to the Ground. They are so Timerous that they never Feed but surrounded with other Beasts that defend them."

Unicorns were even reported in America. In 1673, a scant hundred years prior to the American Revolution, Olfert Dapper wrote:

". . . On the Canadian border there are sometimes seen animals resembling horses, but with cloven hoofs, rough manes, a long straight horn upon the forehead, a curled tail like that of the wild boar, black eyes, and a neck like that of the stag. They live in the loneliest wildernesses and are so shy that the males do not even pasture with the females except in the season of rut, when they are not so wild. As soon as this season is past, however, they fight not only with other beasts but even with those of their own kind."

Certain Explanations of the Unicorn

There appear to be two main sources of the belief in the unicorn as a flesh-and-blood creature: distorted or mistranslated descriptions of real animals and eyewitness accounts of actual unicorns from people who didn't understand what they were seeing.

⚜ The Biblical "One-Horn" ⚜

A lexical misunderstanding was probably the source of the biblical unicorn. The Old Testament Latin scriptures used in the Middle Ages, and the King James Bible that was based on them, came from Greek translations of the original Hebrew sources. The Hebrew word that was eventually translated as "unicorn" was "re'em." It seems likely that the re'em were aurochs—large, strong, dangerous wild cattle. They were a favorite prey of Assyrian hunters, and so they were often shown in the Assyrians' large bas-reliefs—in profile, with only one horn showing. The early Greek translators might have known them as "monokeros," or "one-horn," for this reason. And "one-horn" was duly translated, in the King James Bible, as "unicorn."

❦ Travelers' Tales ❦

"Eyewitness" accounts of unicorns may also be explained. In Tibet, which was long thought to be an abode of unicorns, there is an antelope with two long, straight horns that were reputed to have magical powers. The horns are parallel, looking like a single horn when seen from the side. A herd seen from a distance usually appears to have several one-horned antelopes in it. Travelers from Europe who reached Tibet in medieval times might have seen such a herd, have heard the stories about the animals' horns, and have concluded that they had, at last, seen real unicorns.

For an example of a mistaken traveler, consider this passage from the writings of Marco Polo, as he describes his encounter with "unicorns" in the Far East in the thirteenth century:

"They have wild elephants, and great numbers of unicorns hardly smaller than elephants in size. Their hair is like that of a buffalo, and their feet like those of an elephant. In the middle of their forehead is a very large black horn. Their head is like that of a wild boar, and is always carried bent to the ground. They delight in living in mire and mud. It is a hideous beast to look at, and in no way like what we think and say in our countries. . . . I assure you that it is altogether different from what we fancied."

Based on this detailed description, it seems clear that Marco Polo had not seen magical unicorns, but a herd of rhinoceroses!

Lore of the Unicorn

⚜ The Virgin and the Unicorn ⚜

Medieval and Renaissance descriptions of unicorns were widespread and varied, but most agreed on one thing: No hunter, armed with mere weapons, could take him. But legends abound as to the ability of beautiful young virgins to beguile and tame the wild beast.

If a beautiful young virgin, say the legends, is left alone in a place frequented by a unicorn, the unicorn will run to her as soon as he sees her, lay his head in her lap, and go to sleep. Then the hunters can take him and kill him, or lead him to the palace of the king, where he will be displayed as an emblem of the king's power.

Here is a lovely thirteenth-century love song, written by the poet Thibaut, that captures the essence of this legend:

"The unicorn and I are one:
He also pauses in amaze
Before some maiden's magic gaze,
And while he wonders, is undone.
On some dear breast he slumbers deep
And Treason slays him in that sleep.

Just so have ended my Life's days;
So Love and my Lady lay me low.
My heart will not survive this blow."

Powerful unicorns captured by virgins is a fascinating myth: strength and swiftness overcome by the power of simple innocence. This is the theme of the famous "Unicorn" tapestries, created in fifteenth-century Brussels. The seven tapestries were created as a wedding present. The most famous of the tapestries depicts a beautiful white unicorn chained to a flowering pomegranate tree against a field of millefleurs and is generally interpreted as symbolizing a captured lover.

Of course, not all such stories appeal to our sense of the romantic: The Abyssinian, or Ethiopian, unicorn could be caught by a female monkey, and some stories said that a man, dressed and perfumed like a young woman, could fool a unicorn just as easily.

⚜ The Lion and the Unicorn ⚜

Two beasts were often selected to appear in medieval coats of arms: the lion, symbol of bravery, and the unicorn, symbol of chastity. One of the most enduring myths about unicorns features the pursuit of this chaste beast by a lion. The lion captures his prey after the unicorn impales its horn on a tree. Edmund Spenser retells this story in *The Faerie Queene*:

"Like as a Lyon, whose imperiall powre
A prowd rebellious Unicorne defies,

T'auiode the rash assault and wrathfull stowre
Of his fiers foe, him to a tree applies,
And when him running in ful course he spies,
He slips aside; the whiles that furious beast
His precious horne, sought of his enemies,
Strikes in the stocke, ne thence can be releast,
But to the mighty victour yields a bounteous
feast."

Shakespeare refers to this legend in his poem
"The Rape of Lucrece." He mentions unicorns
in only three places in his plays, and it seems
clear that he did not believe in them. In *Julius*

Caesar, Caesar's gullibility is illustrated by Decius Brutus, who says: "He loves to hear that unicorns may be betrayed with trees."

The lion and the unicorn still appear side-by-side, most commonly in this famous nursery rhyme:

The Lion and the Unicorn were fighting for the
  crown;
The Lion beat the Unicorn all round the town.
Some gave them white bread, some gave them
  brown;
Some gave them plum-cake and drummed them
  out of town.

⚜ A Unicorn's Blessing ⚜

Why was the unicorn myth so powerful in the medieval mind? It certainly was not due to natural science or close observation of living creatures. The legend was far subtler, and in its way, far more real, than mere science.

In medieval times, it was usual for educated people (usually priests) to see everything as an allegory—the physical representation of a spiritual meaning. Even nature was only important as a source of educational and uplifting metaphors. If the facts of nature didn't quite fit the religious requirements, the facts could always be set aside. They were not worth as much, to medieval writers, as the moral truths that might be illustrated by distorting them. And after a while, the distortions took on the weight of fact, copied, repeated, and spread from region to region, from generation to generation.

The unicorn legend was bent to fit allegory as well. The virgin set to catch the unicorn, of course, was Mary; the unicorn was Christ, and his capture by hunters represented the crucifixion. The unicorn's single horn represented Christ's unity with God; the unicorn's fierceness was Christ's fierceness against sin. The unicorn of the bestiaries was small and goatlike, and this represented Christ's meekness and humility.

Perhaps the most enduring aspect of the medieval unicorn was its power as a healer. This comes from descriptions of the unicorn in a medieval bestiary based on Greek sources. In some parts of the world, it says, when animals come down to the water in the evening to drink, they may find snake venom floating on it. The animals sense the poison and wait for the unicorn to appear. The unicorn makes the sign of the cross over the contaminated water with his horn. The water is then safe for all the animals to drink.

This story grew into the most widespread of the unicorn legends. The virgin-capture myth may have been an important religious symbol in the medieval church. But the aspect of the unicorn legend that actually touched people's lives was the mysterious power of its horn.

The Powers of the Horn

❧ The Horn as a Healer ❧

The unicorn's horn had a power that was only hinted at in early writings, which mentioned that kings in India often drank out of cups made of unicorn horn. The cups were said to prevent drunkenness and to have a certain power against poison. By the fifteenth or sixteenth century a far more elaborate story had taken root in Europe.

It began simply. A unicorn's horn, it was said, would "sweat" if it was placed on a table with poisoned food or drink. In those days, poison was an easy way to deal with enemies. Wealthy and powerful men were willing to pay high prices to sailors and travelers for horns, or even pieces of horns, that were said to come from unicorns.

Cups, spoons, and salt cellars were also made of "unicorn's horn" and sold for fabulous prices. The cups were often made of gold or silver, inset with circular slices of "horn."

Very wealthy families often kept a unicorn horn hanging on a chain on the wall in the rooms where feasts were held. At the beginning of the meal, an attendant would carry the horn around the table, touching all the food and drink with it to test for poison. This custom continued at the court of the King of France until 1789. By then, perhaps, no one believed in it, but the old ceremony lingered on until the French Revolution put an end to such frivolous aristocratic ideas.

In the fifteenth and sixteenth centuries, cups and spoons made from "unicorn horn" sold briskly. A few very rich men owned entire horns. So did some religious orders and some cathedrals. The Cathedral of St. Denis, in France, boasted a horn seven feet long, weighing thirteen pounds. One end of the horn was kept in a container of water, and the water was said to bring about miraculous cures. In England, Elizabeth I, James I, and Charles I all owned horns; Elizabeth's was said to be worth 10,000 pounds, then an astonishing amount.

Logically, the unicorn's horn was also thought to have medicinal powers. Scrapings from whole horns were taken rarely and carefully—one rule called for the presence of two men of princely rank as witnesses. But small pieces of unicorn's horn, and powdered horn, were easier to find.

By the end of the sixteenth century, apothecaries would prescribe powdered unicorn horn as a remedy for all poisons, as well as for fevers, mad-dog bites, scorpion stings, epilepsy, worms, and plague. The substance was so widely used that a unicorn, or a unicorn head, became the common symbol of apothecaries' shops in the seventeenth century. Edward Topsell wrote:

". . . The hornes of Unicornes . . . being beaten and drunk in water, doth wonderfully help against poyson: as of late experience doth manifest unto a man, who having taken poison and beginning to swell was preserved by this remedy. I my selfe have herd of a man worthy to be beleeved, that having eaten a poisond cherry, and perceiving his belly to swell, he cured himself by the marrow of this horne being drunk in wine in very short space."

⚜ The Testing of the Horns ⚜

For a time, powder or small pieces of unicorn horn sold for ten times their weight in gold. Whole horns, which were rare, went for twice that.

Owners of unicorn horns devised tests that were said to detect genuine horns. The simplest test was to put the horn in water. If the horn was real, the water would bubble and give off a sound as if it were boiling. True horn, when burned, would give off a sweet smell. The horn could also be put in a covered container with three or four live scorpions. After several hours, the cover would be removed. If the scorpions were dead, that proved the horn was good. Another writer said that all poisonous plants and animals would burst and die when brought near a true unicorn's horn. A spider would die inside a circle drawn with a unicorn's horn, or if it was placed inside the hollow horn.

Some of the writers who described these tests owned unicorn horns themselves and said that they had passed the tests. Very natural, considering how much the owners had paid for the horns—and how much they might hope to get for them later.

Another part of the unicorn that was said to have miraculous powers was the carbuncle, or ruby, that some said could be found in the skull of a unicorn, at the base of its horn. This ruby was considered to be the "king of stones." It could be worn next to the skin as an amulet. Crushed and mixed with wine, it was a remedy for poison, plague, sadness, and nightmares. It was said that a real one shone with its own light in the darkness and could be seen through its wearer's clothing. However, this story never became as widely known as the stories of the powers of the horn itself.

⚜ The Origins of the Horns ⚜

Of course, it is impossible to possess the horn of a unicorn. Where did the unicorn horns sold come from? Many were ivory, taken from an elephant or walrus tusk. The ivory tusk, after being boiled in certain liquids, could be straightened to resemble a unicorn's horn.

Others were not horns at all, but teeth from a real creature that is much more bizarre than a mere unicorn: the narwhal.

Narwhals are small whales, up to eighteen feet in length, that live in the arctic waters of

Greenland and northern Scandinavia. They have only two teeth, both in the upper jaw. In males, one of these two, usually the left, develops into a straight tusk with spiral twists. This tooth can grow as long as nine feet.

There are records indicating that Scandinavian fishermen were hunting narwhals for their horns as early as the twelfth century—and selling the teeth as unicorn horns. They would have done it judiciously, to keep the price up. Once in a while, a horn would wash ashore in Scotland or Wales, and the lucky peasant who found it would become rich.

The Unicorn
in Literature

It is hard, these days, to understand that in the Middle Ages, whether in sacred or secular writings, the unicorn was not a creature of legend. It appeared in stories and poetry much as bears or lions did—very matter-of-factly, and usually only briefly. The powers of the unicorn were a matter for science—such as it was—not for songs and stories. Unicorns were not especially romantic, although they sometimes served as metaphors in love poetry. Usually the poet was the unicorn, trapped and undone by his lady's beauty, just as a unicorn could be trapped and undone by a virgin.

✤ The Arthurian Unicorn ✤

Unicorns appeared, among other places, in an Old French prose romance *Le Chevalier du Papegeau*.

In this story from the fourteenth century, King Arthur finds himself marooned on a strange coast during his first adventure. Near the coast, he finds a dwarf living in a square red tower with no windows or doors.

The dwarf tells King Arthur that he and his wife were stranded there years before, and that his wife died when their son was born. After burying her, the dwarf took the baby and went looking for shelter in a hollow tree. He found an unusually large one and went inside. There he found a number of little creatures that looked like fawns, each with a horn in the center of its forehead. Just then, the mother of the little ones came in—a big, powerful unicorn with a razor-sharp horn. The dwarf hid, but the hungry, frightened baby cried. The mother unicorn took pity on the baby and fed him with her own milk. Soon she befriended the dwarf—feeding him her milk as well, helping him to hunt and build a hut for himself.

The dwarf's baby grew into a giant on his diet of unicorn milk. He built the red tower to protect his father from wild animals. The dwarf tells King Arthur that the mother unicorn still goes everywhere with the young giant. After the dwarf tells his story, Arthur, the dwarf, and the giant have a meal together—the dwarf and Arthur sitting on the top of the tower, and the giant standing next to it. Then the giant and the unicorn drag Arthur's ship off the sands where it had run aground, and they all set sail for England together.

⚜ The Rabelaisian Unicorn ⚜

Rabelais mentions unicorns in Gargannia and *Pantagruel*, published in 1532:

". . . I saw there two-and-thirty unicorns. They are a cursed sort of creature, much resembling a fine horse, unless it be that their heads are like a stag's, their feet like an elephant's, their tails like a wild boar's, and out of each of their foreheads sprouts a sharp black horn, some six or seven feet long. Commonly it dangles down

like a turkey-cock's comb, but when a unicorn
has a mind to fight or put it to any other use,
what does he do but make it stand, and then it
is as straight as an arrow."

✤ Alice and the Unicorn ✤

Not surprisingly, the unicorn makes an appearance in the works of Lewis Carroll, creator of the most delightful whimsy of the Victorian age. In *Through the Looking Glass and What Alice Found There*, Alice encounters a unicorn in a passage that captures the essential paradox of the legendary beast:

". . . He was going on, when his eye happened to fall upon Alice: he turned round instantly, and stood for some time looking at her with an air of the deepest disgust.

'What—is—this?' he said at last.

'This is a child!' Haigha replied eagerly. . . .

'I always thought they were fabulous monsters!' said the Unicorn. 'Is it alive?'

'It can talk,' said Haigha solemnly.

The Unicorn looked dreamily to Alice, and said, 'Talk, child.'

Alice could not help her lips curling into a smile as she began: 'Do you know, I always thought Unicorns were fabulous monsters, too? I never saw one alive before!'

'Well, now we *have* seen each other,' said the Unicorn, 'if you'll believe in me, I'll believe in you. Is that a bargain?' "

⚜ The Living Unicorn ⚜

Unicorns continue in the art and the written
fantasies of today. They are no longer merely
allegories, or proofs against poison. Instead,
they represent a beauty and mystery that come
from beyond our own world, beyond our own
time. This part of the legend has a power, an
inevitability, that let it survive long after the
strained allegories and the quack medicines
were discarded even now, when the true sources
of the legend are "known."

Yet perhaps it is small-minded to be so ready to abandon an old and beautiful legend for mundane facts. Edward Topsell thought so.

"Now our discourse of the Unicorne is of none of these beasts, for there is not any vertue attributed to their hornes, and therefore the vulgar sort of infidell people which scarcely beleeve any hearbe but such as they see in their owne Gardens, or any beast but such as in their own flocks, or any knowledge but such as is bred in their own braines, or any birds which are not hatched in their own Nests, have never made question of these, but of the true Unicorne, whereof ther were more proofes in the world, because of the nobleness of his horne, they have ever bin in doubt. . . ."

What is the truth of the unicorn? A mythical beast? Yes, but a mythical beast that has had more influence over Western culture than most real animals. A symbol? Yes, but a symbol so strong that its meaning can change sharply, and yet the symbol endures.

There may be no delicate hoofprints by the waterside, no flash of white in the moonlit forest, no real horns as relics of wildness betrayed.

Yet in the mind, in dream or fantasy—do you see it? Do you hear it? In the Mountains of the Moon?

The text of this book was set in Sabon by
Harry Chester, Inc. of New York, N.Y.